KB259730

Arthur
Makes the Team

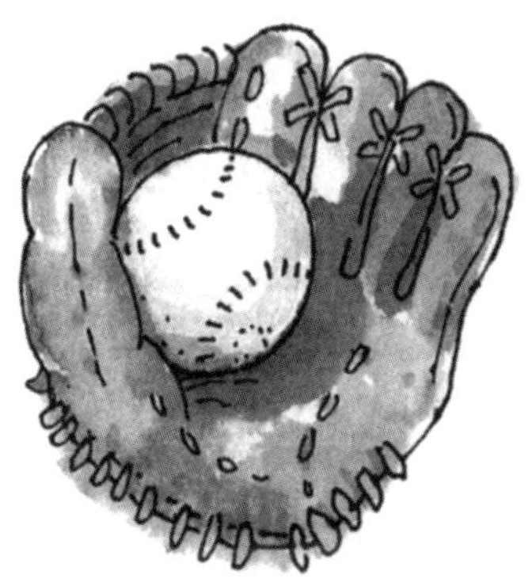

ISBN 978-89-5605-675-3 14740

Longtail Books

For Tucker

Buster and Arthur were walking along the **sidewalk** with their baseball **glove**s. As they walked, they **toss**ed a ball **back and forth**.

"So, do you think you'll be good at baseball?" Buster asked.

Arthur **shrug**ged. "I hope so," he said. He didn't want to **admit** to being **nervous**. He hadn't played last year, like some of the other kids.

"Did you learn a lot last year?" he asked.

Buster laughed. "Did I? Let me show you. Run out for a long catch."

Arthur **trot**ted past a tree.

Buster **wave**d him on. "**Farther** . . . farther . . . Okay, stand there. Are you ready? See if you can catch the famous Buster Ball."

"Ready!" said Arthur. He held up his glove.

Buster threw the ball as hard as he could. But instead of going toward Arthur, the ball **shot** up into a tree. It **bounce**d around in the **branch**es.

"I've got it," said Arthur, circling **underneath**.

The ball bounced down off one branch, then another, before rolling onto a **roof**.

"I've still got it," said Arthur, **follow**ing the ball's every move.

The ball rolled down the roof and into the **gutter**. It shot out the **bottom** of the **downspout**, passed between Arthur's legs, and rolled into a storm **drain**.

"Oops!" said Arthur. "I guess I don't have it **after all**."

Buster looked down the drain. He **sigh**ed. "I lose more balls that way."

"That was a pretty **amazing** throw," said Arthur. "And you learned that in just one season?"

"I sure did. Don't worry—you'll **catch on** quickly. Just think: you're standing out there in the middle of the **field**. There's no one around."

"No one around," said Arthur.

"No place to hide," said Buster.

"No place to hide," Arthur **repeat**ed.

"At the **crack** of the **bat**, the ball is headed your way. Everyone is **staring**, watching your every move."

"My every move?" said Arthur.

"Of course," said Buster. "And not just your team**mate**s. The other team is watching, too. And the **crowd** in the **stand**s. **Especially** your family."

"My family?"

Buster **nod**ded. "Sure. Parents. Grandparents. Sisters. Everybody comes to the games."

Arthur sighed. "Let me **get** this **straight**. I'm all alone in the middle of the field, and the whole world is watching whenever the ball comes to me."

"Pretty **exciting**, huh?" said Buster.

"I guess," said Arthur. *Exciting* wasn't actually the word he had in mind.

"And don't forget batting," said Buster.

"No, I wouldn't want to do that."

Buster **crouch**ed down in a batting **stance**. "It's just you and the **pitcher**. Nothing else **matter**s. You **raise** your bat. Ready. Waiting. The **pitch blaze**s in. You can feel the heat as the ball passes by."

Arthur **swallow**ed. "You feel the heat?"

"Well, maybe not," Buster admitted. "But it's a **tense** moment."

"Because everyone is watching."

"**Exact**ly. The **umpire** calls, 'Strike!' But that's okay. It wasn't your pitch. But now you stand in."

"Stand in," said Arthur.

"It's another fastball. But this time you **swing**. The ball **streak**s like a rocket. It's a home run! You circle the **bases** to the **cheer**s of the crowd."

"**Just like that**?" said Arthur.

"Well, not every time. But it could happen if you're lucky."

Arthur sighed. He didn't know if that would happen to him. But it was nice to think about.

Chapter 2

At the ball **field**, a **bunch** of kids were **huddle**d around the **bulletin board**, looking at the team **roster**s.

"I found my name," said Buster. "Let's see . . . Francine . . . Brain . . . Binky . . . Arthur. Yes! Yes! We're all on the Eagles together. Hey, this is going to be a great team. I can't wait to start **pitch**ing."

"Hey, I want to pitch!" said Francine.

"So do I," said the Brain.

"How will we **choose**?" asked Buster.

"Don't worry," said Francine. "The **coach**

will **decide**."

"But Francine," said the Brain, "your father is the coach."

She smiled. "Funny how these things **work out**."

"How what things work out?" asked her father, coming up to join them. He **had on** his **official** Eagles hat and T-shirt.

"Nothing, Daddy," said Francine, smiling at him.

"I think I'm going to be sick," **whisper**ed Buster.

"I think you'll have **company**," the Brain whispered back.

The whole team—**including** Sue Ellen, Speedy, Fern, and Alex—sat down in the **grass**.

"I'm glad everyone could be here for our first **practice**," said the coach. "As most of you know, I'm Oliver Frensky, Francine's dad."

Francine gave Buster a big smile.

"Now, our **motto** is going to be 'Teamwork!'" the coach went on. "If you have a favorite **position**, you can start with that. But you'll all be moving around. Who's going to be our first **pitcher**?"

Buster, Francine, and the Brain all **raise**d their hands.

"Excellent. We have a whole **staff**. Buster, why don't you go first?"

"But . . . but—," Francine **sputter**ed.

"You'll get your **turn**," her father **reassure**d her.

Everyone else took a position. Arthur **end**ed **up** in right field. Nobody else seemed to want to be there.

"Heads up, everyone!" said the coach, waiting with a **bat** at home plate.* "Go ahead,

---

★ **home plate** [야구 용어] 홈 플레이트. 본루. 주자가 득점하기 위해서 밟아야 하는 오각형 모양의 베이스.

Buster."

Buster **prepare**d to pitch. He **twirl**ed his arm around, **shot** out his leg, and threw as hard as he could.

Coach Frensky **blink**ed.

"Where did the ball go?"

Buster wasn't sure. He was never sure with a Buster Ball. A moment later the ball came down and hit him on the head.

"Are you all right, Buster?" asked the coach.

Buster **nod**ded.

"Good. Try again. But this time **ease** up a little. Don't **wear** your arm out the first day."

Buster nodded. He pitched again—and the ball **sail**ed right over the plate. The coach lined a drive* to Sue Ellen at third **base**.

After a few more pitches, it was Francine's

★ **line a drive** 라인 드라이브를 치다. 라인 드라이브는 공을 타격하여 거의 일직선으로 날아가게 하는 것을 말한다.

turn. Her first pitches were high and outside. Her father **foul**ed them off.

"Nice energy," he said. "Remember now, right over the plate."

Francine's next pitches were better. Her father batted them around the field.

Time for my fastball, thought Francine.

She **grip**ped the ball **firm**ly—and threw.

The ball sailed high over everything—her father, Binky, even the backstop.★

"Well," said her father, "that was certainly over the plate."

"**Way** over," said Binky.

The coach cleared his **throat**. "All right, Francine, let's give someone else a chance."

The Brain took to the mound.✳

"Ready?" asked the coach.

★ **backstop** 그물망. 경기장 밖으로 공이 나가는 것을 방지하고 관중을 보호하기 위해 홈 플레이트 뒤에 설치해 놓은 것.

✳ **mound** [야구 용어] 마운드. 투수가 공을 던질 때 서는 곳.

"In a moment," said the Brain. He **lick**ed his finger and held it up to test the wind **direction**. Then he began **scraping** the mound with his **sneaker**.

"Is everything all right?" asked the coach.

"Oh, yes," said the Brain. **"Proper footing** is very important."

When he was finally ready, the Brain made his first careful pitch.

Coach Frensky hit a grounder* to shortstop.*

The Brain was **please**d. He checked the wind and his footing again. He did that before every pitch, so he didn't get many in.

The last ball went to right field. It was a deep pop fly.*

"I've got it!" said Arthur, moving backward.

★ **grounder** [야구 용어] 땅볼. 지면 위로 굴러가는 볼을 말한다.

✳ **shortstop** [야구 용어] 유격수. 2루와 3루 사이의 지역을 수비하는 내야수.

✳ **pop fly** [야구 용어] 팝 플라이. 타자가 공을 높이 쳐올리는 것을 '플라이' 혹은 '플라이 볼'이라고 하는데, 팝 플라이는 타격한 공이 날아가는 거리가 짧으면서도 높이 뜬 공을 말한다.

He **leap**ed at what he thought was the right moment.

And **miss**ed.

The ball came down behind him.

"Almost!" said the coach. "Arthur, that was a very **graceful** leap."

Graceful? Arthur didn't feel graceful. He could feel his face getting red. He knew everyone was looking at him.

It was starting to look like the season would be a long one.

Chapter 3

Arthur stood in front of his bedroom mirror, **toss**ing a ball up and down in his **mitt**.

His father stopped in the **hall** to watch him. "Ready for your next **practice**, Arthur?" he asked.

Arthur dropped the ball. "Oh, uh . . . yeah," he said.

Mr. Read stepped into the room. "Is everything okay?"

"Um, I guess. Practices have been hard."

"Really? Tell me about them."

"I'm not very **comfortable** yet. The other

day I was playing second **base**. I **field**ed a
sharp grounder but I couldn't get it out of
my **glove**. It was like the ball was **stuck** with
glue."

"What did you do?" his father asked.

"Well, there was a force on at second,
so I took off the glove and threw it to the
shortstop, who was covering the bag.*"

"Was the throw **in time**?"

Arthur **sigh**ed. "The glove was. But the
ball came out along the way and **dribble**d into
the **outfield**. The runner **end**ed **up** at third
base."

"What did the **coach** say?" asked Mr. Read.

"He said I was **ingenious**. Very **creative**.
He uses words like that a lot when I make a
play."

Mr. Read sat down on the bed. "The coach

★ **bag** 베이스(base)의 구어.

has a good eye, Arthur. You just need to give it a little time."

Arthur wasn't so sure. "Everyone else just seems so far ahead of me. And I feel funny asking for help about **stuff** that everybody else knows already."

"Yes, well, most of them played last year, and you didn't. Having a **head start** makes a **difference**. I had kind of the same thing happen to me."

"You did?"

His father **nod**ded. "It was when I first got interested in cooking. Of course, I didn't know I would end up as a **cater**er. I just liked **experiment**ing with food. I was sick the first week and **miss**ed the class where the teacher **explain**ed how all the **equipment** worked. The next week I was too **shy** to ask questions. I just **pretend**ed I knew as much as everyone else."

"Did it work?" asked Arthur.

His father smiled. "For a few minutes. But then we had to make salad **dressing** in a **blend**er. Everyone else knew that the **lid** needed to be **lock**ed a certain way. I didn't. So when I turned it on . . ."

Arthur **gasp**ed.

"You guessed it. The salad dressing ended up on everything and everyone else. It was quite a **mess**."

"Did you get in trouble?"

His father **made a face**. "For a moment I thought my life was over. The teacher was covered in **goop**. He shook his **fist** at me, and goop dropped off his hand onto the **floor**."

Arthur's mouth dropped open.

"The room was perfectly **still**. And then he started to laugh. 'This,' he said, 'is a good **example** of what I was talking about—*last week*.'"

Arthur sighed. "So you **survived**."

"**Exact**ly. But I never tried to pretend I knew what I was doing again. And you shouldn't, either. Don't be **afraid** to ask for help or **advice**. You'll **catch up** soon enough."

Chapter 4

Coach Frensky was standing behind the backstop, watching his team **warm up**.

"Excuse me. Coach?"

The coach turned.

"I'm Buster's mother, Bitsy."

"Nice to meet you. Buster's a fine boy, a real **sparkplug**!"

"That's very nice to hear. I was just **wonder**ing . . . Is the ball very hard?"

"Well, no harder than any baseball."

"I see. I've just been wondering . . . What if it hits Buster?"

"Well, there's always some **risk**, but Buster's very quick. I'm sure—"

"And the baseball hats, are they made of **wool**? I think Buster's **allergic** to wool. If he's **scratch**ing, I don't think he'll be playing his best."

"We'll watch for scratching." Coach Frensky **glance**d at the **bleacher**s. "Now, I'd **recommend** you find a **seat**, um, Bitsy. You don't want all the good ones to be taken."

"Do the seats often **fill up** for **practice**?"

Coach Frensky **hesitate**d. "You never know," he said.

On the **field**, Arthur and Buster were throwing to each other. As Francine **approach**ed, Buster held up an **imaginary microphone** in front of her mouth.

"Excuse me, **Slugger**. Buster here for Action News. Think you'll top your **record** of forty-nine sky balls* today?"

"Very funny," said Francine. "At least my throws go over the plate."

"**Take it easy,**" said Arthur. "You're both on the same team, remember?"

"Stay out of this, Arthur," said Francine. "You need to **concentrate** all your **attention** on holding on to the ball."

"Oh, yeah?" Arthur put his hands on his **hip**s—and the ball dropped out of his **glove**.

Francine laughed and moved onto the field.

"You know what you need, Arthur?" said Buster. "My never-**fail**, always-**succeed**s, one-hundred-percent **guarantee**d, secret good-luck **charm**."

He reached into his pocket and **produce**d a **shrivel**ed **carrot**.

★ sky ball [야구 용어] 높이 뜬 공. 하늘 높이 날아가는 타구. 보통 뜬공을 '플라이 볼(fly ball)'이라고 하는데, 특히 더 높이 올라간 경우 '스카이 볼'이라고 부른다.

Arthur **made a face**.

"Use this and you can't **miss**," said Buster. He handed the carrot to Arthur.

"You're sure about this?" asked Arthur.

"One hundred percent **absolute**ly double-sure guaranteed."

"Okay," said Arthur, and he put it in his pocket.

All during practice, Arthur **finger**ed the good-luck charm. But since no **tough** balls were hit to him, he couldn't be sure if it was working. When Francine came up to **bat**, he **crouch**ed down to be ready.

Francine **crush**ed the next **pitch** to deep right field. Arthur ran back, watching it the whole way.

"Watch the **fence!**" Buster **yell**ed.

Arthur **stop**ped **short** and looked up. The ball was coming down. He reached out to catch it.

The ball **bounce**d off his glove and went over the fence.

"Home run!" shouted Francine, rounding the **base**s.

Arthur **frown**ed.

Later, Arthur returned the carrot to Buster.

"Here," he said. "I think it's broken. Or maybe it's **run out of** luck."

Then he walked away.

Buster **examine**d the carrot and **shrug**ged. He took a **bite** and put the rest in his pocket.

After **practice**, **Coach** Frensky **led** the team to the Sugar Bowl.

"You've been working hard," he said. "Time for a little **reward**."

Arthur was the last in, just behind Buster. It was **amazing** to him that everyone else could be so happy and **relax**ed. Most of the kids had made the same kind of **mistake**s on the **field** that he had. **Somehow** it didn't seem to **bother** them so much.

"A great practice **deserve**s ice cream!" said the coach. He went off to see about getting some tables pushed together.

"Are you **prepare**d, Arthur?" Francine asked.

Arthur eyed her **cautious**ly. "What do you mean?"

"An ice cream cone can be **tricky**. If you're not careful, you might drop it."

A lot of the kids laughed.

"Don't listen to her, Arthur," said Buster. "You're **entitle**d to ice cream just as much as the rest of us. If you want, though, I'll hold it for you."

"Thanks, Buster," said Arthur. "I think."

Once their **order**s were taken, everyone sat down. Arthur, Francine, Buster, the Brain, and Binky were all at the same table.

Francine was busy **complain**ing. "Our problem is **bat**ting," she said. "We don't have good batting."

Arthur had **struck out** twice that afternoon.

He was **swing**ing too soon, the coach had told him.

"I think we look pretty good," said Buster.

Francine laughed. "With your **eyesight**, I'm not **surprise**d."

"There's nothing wrong with my eyesight," said Buster. "I eat **plenty** of **carrot**s."

Arthur **fiddle**d with his glasses. Sometimes it was hard to **keep his eye on** the ball.

"Some people," said Binky, "have to learn how to stop the ball." He **pound**ed his **chest**. "Even if you can't keep it in your **glove**, you keep it in front of you."

Arthur looked down at his legs. Balls had passed through them so often, they felt like **goalpost**s.

"If we **concentrate** on learning the **fundamental**s," said the Brain, "our chances of winning will **improve** over time."

"I **suppose**," said Francine. "But they don't

look too good right now."

"Well," said the Brain, "it would help if you stopped throwing the ball over Fern's head."

"I didn't do that!" said Francine. "And she was standing too close, anyway."

Coach Frensky **arrive**d at the table with two **pitcher**s of **soda**.

"Hey!" he said, **frown**ing. "I don't want to hear any talk like that. We're a team, remember?"

Everyone **shut up**.

Coach Frensky **survey**ed the table. "Where's Arthur?" he asked.

"He was here a second ago," said Buster.

"Probably went for napkins," said Binky.

"Look!" said the Brain. He pointed out the window.

Arthur was **slink**ing up the street. A line of **drip**s from his ice cream cone **trail**ed behind him.

THE SUC

"I guess he wasn't in the **mood** for talk," said Francine.

"I guess not," said her father. But he stood there thinking it over for a long time.

Chapter 6

At dinner, Arthur sat quietly at the table. He **barely** touched his hamburger. He wasn't very hungry.

The same could not be said for D.W. Her hamburger was half gone, and she was **munch**ing away on corn-on-the-cob.★

"I see you **favor** the rolling **approach**," said her father.

D.W. looked **confuse**d. "What's that?"

"It's when you roll your corn around

★ **corn-on-the-cob** 옥수숫대(cob)에 붙어 있는 옥수수(corn).

before moving it down a little and rolling it some more."

D.W. stopped to look at her corn. "It's the best way," she said.

"Don't be so sure," said her mother. "Some people favor the **typewriter** approach—eating **all the way** across in a **row**, turning the **cob** a little, and then starting a new row."

D.W. **shrug**ged. "My way is better," she said.

"For you, sweetie," said her mother.

"What do you think, Arthur?" asked Mr. Read.

"Huh?"

Arthur hadn't been listening.

"Which way do you like to eat corn?" his father asked.

Arthur **sigh**ed. "Whichever way you make the fewest **mistake**s."

Mr. Read looked confused. "I'm not sure

you can make a mistake eating corn," he said. "True, you could **miss** a **kernel** here or there, but I'm not sure that really **count**s."

"Arthur's not talking about corn," said D.W. "He's talking about baseball."

"How are your **practice**s going?" asked his mother.

"Not too well," said Arthur. "I know what to do in my head. But my body doesn't always go along."

"That's perfectly **natural**," said Mr. Read. "Be **patient**, Arthur. You're paying **attention**, and that's what's important. Baseball is ninety-nine percent **concentration**."

"Sometimes it feels like everyone is concentrating on what a bad job I'm doing. Not **Coach** Frensky, though. He's always **encouraging**. He says I'm making good **progress**."

"Which parts do you feel **comfortable**

with?" asked his mother.

Arthur stopped to think. "I can throw okay. And when the ball is hit to me, I can get to the right place . . ."

"But you can't catch the ball," said D.W.

"D.W.!" said her father. "You'll catch more than a ball if you say another word."

D.W. went back to her corn.

Arthur **stare**d at his plate. "She's right," he said. "It's what everyone else says."

"**Nonsense**," said Mr. Read. "I'm sure you're making a **positive contribution**. There are probably people talking about it even now."

"You really think so?"

Mr. Read **nod**ded. "**Absolute**ly. So you'd better **eat up**. Ballplayers need their **strength**."

Arthur nodded. With their first game coming up, he wanted to be ready. He picked up his corn in both hands. With a look at D.W., he began eating it across in rows.

Chapter 7

"It's **painful**," Francine was saying. She was sitting in her living room with Muffy.

"What's painful?" Muffy asked. "No, don't tell me. It **has something to do with** baseball."

Francine was **surprise**d. "How did you know?" she asked.

"Because that's all you talk about **lately**. Double plays* . . . making the cutoff* . . .

★ **double play** [야구 용어] 더블 플레이. 2명의 선수가 한꺼번에 아웃시키는 일.

✲ **cutoff** [야구 용어] 커트오프. 외야에서 홈으로 보내는 공을 내야수가 중간에 차단하는 일.

guarding the plate."

"Well, it's important," said Francine.

Muffy **yawn**ed. "Not to me. I could understand it better if you thought your team was **any good**."

Francine **punch**ed her **pillow**. "Don't **remind** me. Buster can't throw. The Brain takes too long for everything. And **as for** Arthur . . ." She shook her head.

"Couldn't you **promote** him or something?" said Muffy. "Make him **president** or **general** manager? Anything to get him off the **field**. My daddy's always talking about people getting **kick**ed **upstairs** in business."

Francine hadn't thought of that. "It might work. We could give Arthur lots of interesting jobs. He'd be really busy."

"Give him a **fancy** title and some **fringe benefit**s," said Muffy. "You know, like free **park**ing and paid **vacation**s. My daddy says those are important."

Francine was **nod**ding. "Yes, yes," she said. "Arthur would probably like all that."

"Arthur would probably like *what?*" asked her father, coming in from the kitchen.

"We were just **discuss**ing the team, Daddy."

The **coach** smiled. "We're **pull**ing **together** nicely," he said. "Still a few **kink**s, of course, but that's only **normal**."

Francine smiled at him. "Speaking of kinks, Daddy, Muffy **suggest**ed a way to get Arthur off the field: promote him to **assistant** coach."

"Oh, really?" said Mr. Frensky.

Francine **fold**ed her fingers together. "What do you say, Daddy? Please! I can't even throw straight because I'm worrying what **dumb** thing Arthur's going to do next."

"That sounds serious," said her father. "You're worried about Arthur, aren't you?"

"Why,* yes . . . Can't you see that?"

Her father **stroke**d his **chin**. "It's **natural** for you to be **concern**ed. **After all**, he is one of your best friends."

"Then you'll do it?"

Her father thought for a moment. "As coach, I have to look **beyond** any one player's needs. I have to **consider** the whole team."

"Of course," said Francine. "I think the whole team would benefit."

"You have to stand way back to get the big picture," said her father. "I may not have been seeing everything myself. Thank you, Francine."

"So you'll promote him?"

Her father shook his head. "No, no, I've got a better idea."

"Oh?" Francine didn't want a better idea.

★ **why** 오, 아니, 이런, 어머. 이유를 묻는 '왜'라는 의문사가 아니라, 놀라거나 의외라는 반응을 나타내는 감탄사로 쓰였다.

She liked her idea just the way it was.

Her father **rub**bed his chin. "Yes . . . **definite**ly a better idea. I'm not going to promote Arthur. I'm going to promote you instead."

"What? You mean you want to get me off the field?"

"Not **exact**ly," said her father, **grin**ning **broad**ly. "I had a different **promotion** in mind."

Francine looked at him **suspicious**ly. Whenever her father used that **tone**, something **odd was bound to** happen.

Chapter 8

Arthur stood in his **garage**, throwing a tennis ball against the wall.

***Bounce**-bounce-catch.*

Bounce-bounce-catch.

Too bad they don't use these in the games, he thought.

"Hi, Arthur."

Francine stood in the **driveway**.

Arthur **ignore**d her.

Bounce-bounce-catch.

Bounce-bounce-catch.

"Come on, Arthur. You can't ignore me

forever."

Arthur stopped bouncing the ball.

"What brings you here, Francine? No, don't tell me. I'll **bet** you've **thought up** some new **insult**s since yesterday."

Francine's face **redden**ed. "Actually, I came over with some news. My father has made me the new **assistant coach**."

"**Congratulation**s. Would that be Assistant Coach **in Charge of Criticism**?"

"No, no . . . Look, Arthur, maybe I have gotten a little **carried away lately**. I'm sorry. But now my dad says I have to make sure the team works together."

She took out a baseball.

"And my first project is you."

"Me?" Arthur **cross**ed his arms. "What if I don't want to be a project?"

"Would you rather be **tease**d and feel **embarrass**ed all the time?"

Arthur **sigh**ed. He picked up his **glove**, and they went into the **backyard**.

"Ready?" said Francine.

She threw the ball high **overhead**.

Arthur circled **underneath** it. "I've got it! I've got it!"

The ball **land**ed five feet* away.

Francine **smother**ed a **giggle**. "Let's try again," she said.

She picked up the ball and threw it up into the air.

Arthur **raise**d his glove.

"That's it," said Francine. "Get under it!"

Arthur **follow**ed the ball's **path**—until the sun **blind**ed him. He raised his arm to **block** the sun—and the ball hit him on the head.

"Ouch!"

"Well," said Francine, "at least you were

★**feet** 길이의 단위 피트. 1피트는 약 30.48센티미터이다.

under it. Look." She came over to show him. "Use your glove to keep the sun out of your eyes. That also puts the glove in a better place to catch the ball. Don't think about doing everything at once. Break it into steps."

"Oh," said Arthur. "I see."

"One more time . . ."

She threw the ball up again. This time Arthur used his glove to block the sun. He circled and circled—and caught the ball.

Arthur smiled.

Francine smiled, too.

They **practice**d a few more times.

"I think you're **get**ting **the hang of** this, Arthur."

He thought so, too.

"Thanks, Francine. You know, you might take a little **advice** yourself."

"Me? About what?"

"About **pitch**ing your fastball." He

crouched down into a catching **stance**. "Come on, **fire** it in here."

Francine threw the ball. It **sail**ed over Arthur's head, Pal's doghouse, and the **fence**.

While Francine went to get the ball, Arthur stopped to think.

"All right," said Francine, returning to her **position**. "Let's try again."

"Wait a minute," said Arthur. "You know, Francine, maybe you should think about your pitching the same way you told me to think about my catching?"

"What do you mean?"

"Breaking it into steps. Look, when you throw, you need to push off with your legs first and use your shoulder. And even after you **release** the ball, you still have to **follow through**."

"How do you know so much about it?"

Arthur looked a little embarrassed.

"Well?"

"Actually, it was D.W. I heard her **explain**ing the whole thing to my mother."

"You're telling me to take advice from D.W.?"

Arthur **shrug**ged. "Nobody has to know— **especially** D.W. What have you got to lose?"

"All right," said Francine. She got ready.

"Legs . . . shoulder . . ."

She fired the ball in at Arthur.

"Ouch!" he shouted. He pulled his hand out of his glove and shook it. "That was a real fastball."

Francine looked **please**d. "It was, wasn't it?" she said. "Thanks for the **tip**."

"You're welcome," said Arthur.

Francine **pause**d. "I really am sorry I teased you so much before."

Arthur **nod**ded. "Well, you do **overdo** it sometimes."

"If I ever overdo it again, let me know. **Deal**?"

"Deal."

"It was kind of your **fault**, though."

"My fault?" said Arthur. "How do you **figure** that?"

"Well, if you hadn't kept dropping balls, I wouldn't have teased you."

"Oh, yeah? Well at least when I throw a ball, it lands in the same **neighborhood**."

As Francine started to answer, she suddenly **froze**—and laughed.

Arthur laughed, too. "Here we go again . . . ," he said.

Chapter 9

Coach Frensky **paced back and forth** in front of his bench. "Okay, team, this is our first game. The Penguins are pretty good, I hear." He took a deep **breath**. "But I want you to play just the way you have in **practice**. Just go out and have fun."

The coach **clap**ped his hands. "Okay, team. Let's go!"

The Eagles took the **field**. In the first inning,* a ball was hit **sharp**ly on the ground

---

★ **inning** [야구 용어] 이닝. 한 회, 양 팀이 공격과 수비를 한 번씩 끝내는 동안을 말한다.

to Arthur. He fielded it cleanly and threw to second **base**.

"All right, Arthur!" said Buster.

His parents **cheer**ed from the **bleacher**s.

"That's my brother," D.W. told everyone around her. "I taught him everything he knows."

The next four innings passed quickly. Each team scored two **run**s. In the bottom* of the fifth, Arthur came up to **bat** for the second time. He had walked before.

Now he **rap**ped a single* to center.

"Way to go, Arthur!" **yell**ed Francine from the bench.

Buster was next. He **foul**ed off two **pitch**es but **swung all the way** around on the third.

"Strike three!" shouted the **umpire**.

★ **bottom** [야구 용어] 한 회의 말(末).
＊ **single** [야구 용어] 단타, 1루타.

Mrs. Baxter stood up in the **stand**s and clapped. "Way to swing, Buster!" she called out.

The Brain pitched the last two innings. The sixth was **scoreless**, but in the top★ of the seventh, the Penguins scored a run to take the **lead**. Then, with one out, their fifth **batter** singled to first and reached third on an overthrow.✳

The next batter came up.

The Brain **lick**ed his finger, testing the wind **direction**.

Then he threw to the plate.

Thwack!

It was a deep fly ball.✳

"It's yours, Arthur," Francine called from

★ **top** [야구 용어] 한 회의 초(初).

✳ **overthrow** [야구 용어] 오버스로. 악송구. 공을 너무 높거나 멀리 보내 야수가 잡기에 어려운 공.

✳ **fly ball** [야구 용어] 플라이 볼. 뜬공. 높이 날아가는 타구. 평범한 플라이 볼은 수비수에 잡혀서 아웃이 되는 경우가 많다.

second base.

"I can't watch," said Buster in left field.

Arthur **backpedal**ed over the **grass**. He **blink**ed a few times, but he never took his eye off the ball. Remember what Francine said, he told himself. He **shield**ed his eyes with his glove.

Arthur reached the **fence**. The ball was coming down fast.

Plopp.

Arthur had caught it.

"**Relay**!" shouted Francine.

Arthur threw the ball. Francine caught it and **spun** around. The runner had tagged up* at third and was heading for home plate.

Binky was waiting.

"Throw it!" he called out.

★ **tag up** [야구 용어] 태그 업. 타자가 친 공이 플라이 볼(fly ball)일 때, 주자가 베이스를 밟은 상태에 있다 수비팀이 그 공을 잡는 순간, 다음 베이스를 향해 달려가는 동작을 말한다.

Francine wasn't pitching, but she knew she had to throw a perfect fastball. She **plant**ed her feet **firm**ly and **fire**d to him.

The runner was **sliding** in. Binky **swept** him with the tag.*

"Out!" called the umpire.

Arthur's team **trot**ted in from the field. They were down one run, but they still had their last **turn** at bat.

The game wasn't over yet.

★ **tag** [야구 용어] 태그. 수비자가 주자에게 볼을 대서 아웃시키는 일. 야수가 날아온 공을 확실하게 잡은 상태에서 베이스나 주자를 터치하는 동작을 말한다.

Everyone on the bench was watching the **field**.

Sue Ellen was up first. The first **pitch** was a ball.*

"Wait for yours!" shouted Francine.

Sue Ellen **nod**ded. She stepped back into the **batter**'s box.

In came the pitch.

Sue Ellen **swung** hard—and lined the ball into left field.

★ **ball** [야구 용어] 볼. 스트라이크 존을 통과하지 않은 투구 또는 땅에 닿은 투구로, 타자가 치지 않은 공을 말한다.

Coach Frensky **whistle**d. "All right! The **tie**ing run's on first."

Fern was the next batter. She hit a blooper★ to right field, **advancing** Sue Ellen to second.

"Keep it going," said the coach.

Now Binky came to the plate. He **tap**ped the **dirt** from his **cleat**s and **cock**ed his **bat**.

In came the pitch.

Binky swung hard, but a little early. The ball went deep to right field, but it was caught just before the **fence**. He was out, but Sue Ellen tagged up at second and ran to third.

Buster was up next.

"Just make good **contact**," said the coach. "A single ties it. Keep us alive."

Buster nodded.

He watched the first two pitches pass. One

★blooper [야구 용어] 블루퍼. 힘없이 높이 뜬 플라이 볼.

ball and one strike.

The third pitch came in. Buster jumped on it.

The ball **pop**ped up a mile★ high. Everyone looked up.

The **pitcher** called for the catch.

Arthur held his **breath**. Maybe the pitcher would **trip** on the **grass** or be **blind**ed by the sun or get a sudden **itch** in his back and **scratch** it with his **glove**.

Thummp!

The ball was caught. The game was over. The Penguins had won.

Buster **trudge**d back to the **dugout** as the other team ran off the field, **cheer**ing in **victory**.

"Good **effort**, Buster," said the coach. "I thought that one was heading for the fence."

★**mile** 거리의 단위 마일. 1마일은 약 1.60934킬로미터이다.

"Me, too," said Arthur. "Good try."

Francine **storm**ed over to Buster. "Boy,[*]
Buster, all we needed was one little hit, and
you couldn't—"

Arthur **cough**ed.

Francine looked at him. "—and you
couldn't . . . have made a better try. Good
job."

She **pat**ted Buster on the shoulder.

Their families **gather**ed round for a few
minutes before everyone headed home.

Arthur, Francine, and Buster were the last
to leave. They **replay**ed the whole game in
their minds.

"We really did pretty well," said Arthur.
"And the season's just starting."

"That's right," said Francine. "The next
game will be better."

★ **boy** 어머나, 맙소사. 일반적으로 알고 있는 '소년'이라는 의미가 아니라, 놀라움과
안타까움을 나타내는 감탄사로 쓰였다.

Buster **shrug**ged. "I hope so," he said.

"You know, Buster," said Arthur, "Francine gave me some baseball **tip**s the other day. Maybe she could do the same for you."

"I don't know . . . ," said Buster.

"Just think about all the power you put into your Buster Ball," said Francine.

Buster **brighten**ed.

"We just need to find a way to get that power into your bat. We'll have to **get together** and—"

"What about now?" Buster asked.

"Now?" Francine looked around. The field was **empty**.

Buster **grab**bed a bat and went to home plate. "Come on, come on, what are you waiting for?"

"Arthur?" **whisper**ed Francine.

"Yes?"

"Thanks for stopping me before I **tease**d

Buster the way I teased you."

"You're welcome. And thanks for helping me with my game. See? Teamwork is the answer."

Francine nodded. "Yeah. But you know, soccer season is coming up. And if you **stink** at that, I get to tease you all over again."

With that, she went to the **pitcher**'s mound, leaving Arthur to go behind the plate.

"All right, Buster, pay **attention**. First thing we do . . ."

Arthur smiled. He wouldn't say that Francine would *never* learn.

But it **definite**ly was going to take some time.